Organic
DISCIPLES

—— STUDY GUIDE ——

BOOKS IN THE ORGANIC OUTREACH TRILOGY

Organic Outreach for Ordinary People
Organic Outreach for Churches
Organic Outreach for Families

BOOKS BY KEVIN AND SHERRY HARNEY

Organic Disciples
No Is a Beautiful Word
Praying with Eyes Wide Open
Leadership from the Inside Out
Seismic Shifts
Finding a Church You Can Love
The U-Turn Church (with Bob Bouwer)
Reckless Faith
Empowered by His Presence

Organic DISCIPLES

STUDY GUIDE

SEVEN WAYS TO GROW SPIRITUALLY AND NATURALLY SHARE JESUS

Kevin G. Harney

Sherry Harney

ZONDERVAN REFLECTIVE

ZONDERVAN REFLECTIVE

Organic Disciples Study Guide
Copyright © 2021 by Kevin Harney and Sherry Harney

Requests for information should be addressed to:
Zondervan, *3900 Sparks Dr. SE, Grand Rapids, Michigan 49546*

Zondervan titles may be purchased in bulk for educational, business, fundraising, or sales promotional use. For information, please email SpecialMarkets@Zondervan.com.

ISBN 978-0-310-13908-9 (softcover)
ISBN 978-0-310-13909-6 (ebook)

Cover design: RAM Creative
Cover photo: © Zen Chung / Pexels
Interior design: Denise Froehlich

Printed in the United States of America

21 22 23 24 25 LSC 10 9 8 7 6 5 4 3 2 1

Contents

How to Use This Guide

The *Organic Disciples Study Guide* is designed to be experienced in a group setting such as a Bible study, Sunday school class, or any small group gathering. Each session begins with a welcome section and a question to get you thinking about the topic. You will then watch a video teaching and engage in a small-group discussion, including several readings from the Bible. You will close each session with a key Scripture and a time of reflection and prayer as a group.

Each person in the group should have a copy of this study guide and a Bible. Whatever translation you have is fine. You are also encouraged to have a copy of the *Organic Disciples* book, because reading it alongside this study guide will provide you with deeper insights and make the journey more meaningful.

To get the most out of your group experience, keep the following points in mind. First, the real growth in this study will happen during your small-group time. This is where you will process the content of the teaching for the week, ask questions, and learn from others as you hear what God is doing in their lives. For this reason, it is important for you to be fully committed to the group and attend each session so you can build trust and rapport with the other members. If you choose only to go through the motions, or if you refrain from participating, there is less of a chance you will find what you're looking for during this study.

Second, remember that the goal of your small group is to serve as a place where people can share, learn about God, and build intimacy and friendship. For this reason, seek to make your group a safe place. This means being honest about your thoughts and feelings and listening carefully to everyone else's opinion. (If you are a group leader, additional instructions and resources for leading productive group discussions are included at the back of this study guide.)

Third, resist the temptation to fix a problem someone might be having or to correct his or her theology, because that's not the purpose of your small-group time. Also, keep everything your group shares confidential. Doing so will foster a rewarding sense of community in your group and create a place where people can heal, be challenged, and grow spiritually.

Following your group time, reflect on the material you've covered by engaging in the between-sessions activities following each session called "Adventures in Organic Discipleship." These are provided for you to use between sessions to dig deeper into the material. Each of these sections provides you with four practical and life-changing ideas to help you grow as a disciple. For each session, you may wish to complete the personal study all in one sitting or spread it out over a few days. Note that if you are unable to finish (or even start!) your between-sessions personal study, you should still attend the group study session. You are still wanted and welcome at the group.

Keep in mind that the videos, discussion questions, and activities are simply meant to kick-start your thoughts so you are open not only to what God wants you to hear but also to how to apply it to your life. As you go through this study, be listening and open to what God is saying to you as you learn how to grow as an organic disciple of Jesus.

> **Note:** If you are a group leader, additional resources are provided at the back of this guide to help you lead your group members through the study.

Introduction

Kermit the Frog and Miss Piggy. Salt and pepper. Mickey Mouse and Minnie. Peas and carrots. Mario and Princess Peach (of Nintendo fame). Some things just go together, hand in glove.

Loving Jesus *and* sharing his grace with the world should be at the top of the pairing list when it comes to the Christian life. When we grow as disciples, our hearts become more like Jesus' heart, and our Savior's heart is always for lost and wandering sheep.

When the leaders of the religious establishment of his day asked Jesus, "Which is the greatest commandment in the Law?" without skipping a beat, our Savior said, "'Love the Lord your God with all your heart and with all your soul and with all your mind.' This is the first and greatest commandment. And the second is like it: 'Love your neighbor as yourself'" (Matt. 22:36–39).

Grow in love with God (discipleship), and love your neighbor with God's heart (evangelism). For some reason Christians can miss this beautiful and essential pairing established by our God from the very beginning. Every part of our spiritual journey should draw us closer to the heart of Jesus. As this happens, the Holy Spirit propels us outward with God's grace to those who are broken, hurting, rebellious, and wandering.

Over the past thirty years, we have had the honor of equipping Christians to organically share their faith in ways that feel natural to them and to the people with whom they share. From New Zealand to El Salvador, from the Netherlands to cities all over the United States, we have heard a recurring theme. Every day Christians, pastors, and denominational leaders have asked us to build a bridge between discipleship and evangelism. It seems like almost every follower of Jesus believes that growth as disciples should make us more like Jesus and also naturally lead us into the world with his good news. Christian pastors believe that a natural byproduct of equipping their congregational members to follow the Savior should be dynamic and church-changing evangelistic activity. Denominational leaders seek to develop discipleship strategies that also kindle the fires of revival.

Here's the problem. It is simply not happening! It is sad to say, but we have heard the brokenhearted refrain from passionate followers of Jesus around the world. "We are discipling people well, but it is not leading to gospel sharing activity." They say, "We are watching believers grow in knowledge of the Scriptures, prayer, worship, and other aspects of spiritual growth, but they are not naturally sharing the good news of the Savior they love."

The eight-session study you are beginning is a journey of discovery of how discipleship and evangelism should exist in a perfect partnership. When we grow in Christlikeness, our heart for the world should expand. As we follow the Savior more closely, we walk with him into the world he loves and we share his good news. When we love Jesus with increasing passion, we grow to love those he came to save.

Our prayer is that these eight sessions will help you connect your journey of discipleship with a passion for the world to meet the Savior you know and love. As you study Jesus' life, become more like him, and mature in faith, may the Spirit of the living God propel you into the mission field that is right next door and at the ends of the earth. May discipleship and evangelism be so fused together in your mind, heart, and life that every step you take with Jesus leads you to the people he died to save.

WITH YOU ON THE JOURNEY,
KEVIN AND SHERRY HARNEY

Foundations

Three Epic Questions

Inspired by the Holy Spirit, the apostle Paul wrote these words to Timothy, a young pastor who was seeking to give leadership to the church in the ancient city of Ephesus: "And the things you have heard me say in the presence of many witnesses entrust to reliable people who will also be qualified to teach others" (2 Tim. 2:2).

After Jesus rose from the dead and before he ascended to heaven, he told his followers, "All authority in heaven and on earth has been given to me. Therefore go and make disciples of all nations, baptizing them in the name of the Father and of the Son and of the Holy Spirit, and teaching them to obey everything I have commanded you. And surely I am with you always, to the very end of the age" (Matt. 28:18–20).

These are the final words of Jesus recorded in Matthew's Gospel.

— Welcome —

Theirs is a marriage made in heaven.

It was love at first sight.

They are soul mates.

What a perfect couple!

Writers, storytellers, and moviemakers through the ages have tried to capture the glory of the perfect couple—from Romeo and Juliet to Rhett Butler and Scarlett O'Hara (*Gone with the Wind*) to Lucy and Ricky Ricardo (*I Love Lucy*) to Katniss Everdeen and Peeta Mellark (*The Hunger Games*). In almost every case there is drama, tension, intrigue, and conflict. Relationships are complex and never seem to go as smoothly as we would hope.

What is true in the stories told through the centuries is also true of the story that God is writing in the lives of his children today. God wants to wed in our souls and connect in our daily lives two powerful and world-changing ideas. The problem is, we often see them as divorced from each other or at odds with one another.

Here are the two epic partners in this divine marriage plan:

- **Discipleship:** Discipleship is the journey of becoming like Jesus, growing in spiritual maturity, and helping others to do the same. We make this journey on our own and in community with other believers.
- **Evangelism:** Evangelism is the adventure of sharing the grace and love of Jesus Christ, the risen Lord, and the message of salvation in him. We go on this adventure in our personal lives and in partnership with God's people.

Too often we see these two ideas as rivals. But God sees them as inseparably bound together. What we will learn as we immerse ourselves in organic discipleship is that:

- Discipleship and evangelism are not enemies.
- Discipleship and evangelism are not just friends.
- Discipleship and evangelism are marriage partners.

Let's never treat these two God-given callings as if they are at odds with each other. Let's recognize that even friendship is not a strong enough idea to characterize their relationship. May God help us see discipleship and evangelism as marriage partners joined in the sight and heart of God. What God has joined together, let no person tear apart.

— Share —

How have you seen people or churches lift up one of these two powerful callings (discipleship and evangelism) but spend less attention on the other?

> The future of the church requires leaders
> who recognize that true discipleship
> moves people out with the gospel.

— Watch —

Play the video for session 1 of the *Organic Disciples* small group experience. (These are free at www.OrganicDisciples.org/SmallGroupResources.) As you watch, use the following outline to record any thoughts, questions, or key points that stand out to you.

How can I know I am growing as a disciple?

- The essential place of the fruit of the Spirit

- Markers of spiritual maturity

- Every ingredient is needed.

Is discipleship bigger than my relationship with Jesus? Yes!

- The power of four generations
  - Generation 1

  - Generation 2

  - Generation 3

  - Generation 4

> Discipleship happens every time one believer takes the hand of another and helps them move closer to Jesus.

What is the relationship between discipleship and evangelism?

- What we mean by discipleship

- Connecting the dots between discipleship and evangelism

—— Discuss ——

With your group, discuss what you have just watched and explore these concepts in Scripture. Use the following questions to guide your discussion.

1. Tell about a person God has used in your life to disciple you (help you take consistent steps toward becoming more like Jesus). How do you feel about this person and how they have influenced your life?

2. **Read:** Galatians 5:22–23. Why is the fruit of the Spirit essential as we grow in the markers of maturity? What dangers might we encounter if we are growing in the markers but do not exhibit the fruit of the Spirit?

> When the fruit of the Spirit blossoms in us, every aspect of our spiritual lives is strengthened.

3. What are some of the actions, attitude changes, and spiritual practices that you have discovered help you grow in the fruit of the Spirit? What one step will you take to grow the fruit of the Spirit in the coming month?

4. **Read:** Ephesians 4:14–16. What are some of the results of seeking to grow up in faith and become a mature disciple of Jesus?

5. What seems to get in the way of consistent spiritual growth? What can we do to overcome such obstacles?

> When we are developing each of the seven markers, we move upward toward God, inward toward his family, and outward with the good news of Jesus.

6. **Read:** 2 Timothy 2:2. Tell about a person you are seeking to influence to draw closer to Jesus and walk in a richer and more dynamic relationship with the Savior. What are you doing to help this person grow? How is it going?

7. When we see discipleship as *any effort* to help another person grow in faith and walk more intimately with Jesus, what are some of the activities and actions we can take that can be considered discipleship? (Try to make a rapid-fire list of at least twenty things, because otherwise the list could go on and on.)

8. A serious spiritual battle seems to keep believers from seeing the beautiful marriage of discipleship and evangelism. Why do you think the enemy would want believers to keep these callings separate?

9. Which of these two God-given callings do you most naturally gravitate toward? Which one needs a bit more attention in your life? How can your group pray for you as you prepare to go deeper in both of these areas to wed them in your heart and life?

READ AND REFLECT

Each session, you will be given a key verse to learn from one of the passages covered in the video teaching. This week, your suggested verse is 2 Timothy 2:2:

> And the things you have heard me say in the presence of many witnesses entrust to reliable people who will also be qualified to teach others.
>
> **—2 TIMOTHY 2:2**

Silently or as a group, read this verse three or four times. What is its message? Consider committing this verse to memory over the next week.

RESPOND

When you think of all you have learned in this session about the foundations of discipleship and evangelism, what is one big lesson that has locked into your heart or one specific action that will impact your life?

PRAY

Close your group time by praying in any of the following directions:

- Ask the Holy Spirit to grow his fruit in your heart and life so that each step of growth in spiritual maturity you take will be guided by him and never lead to spiritual arrogance.
- Pray that each marker of Christian maturity will increase in your life as you walk with Jesus and grow up in faith.
- Thank God for specific people he has placed in your life who have helped you grow closer to Jesus and increase in maturity as a child of God.
- Invite God to lead people into your life whom you can disciple by helping them grow in faith and walk more closely with the Savior.

- Ask Jesus to help you grow deeper in faith and become more like him so that you can naturally join him on his mission of sharing his love and truth with the world every single day of your life.

The dream of organic disciples is to help Christians

mature in Jesus and shine his light in the world every

step of the journey—for every believer, whatever

their age or place of spiritual development, to carry

God's grace, truth, and good news to the world.

Adventures in Organic Discipleship

Go deeper into the material you have covered in this session by engaging in the following between-session learning experiences. Each week, you will find four practical and life-impacting experiences you can engage in to go deeper as a disciple.

— Learn More (Growing your mind as a disciple) —

LESSONS FROM JESUS' EARLY FOLLOWERS

Read the following passages and take note of what you learn from Jesus' calling of and instructions for some of his early followers:

Matthew 4:18–22

Matthew 8:18–22

Matthew 9:9–13

John 21:15–19

—— Live More (Developing spiritual disciplines) ——

THE DISCIPLINE OF LISTENING

Ask God some good questions about the things you are learning from the Scriptures in this study. Wait quietly and listen for his whispers and nudges and the impressions he places on your heart. It might be a Scripture verse the Holy Spirit brings to mind. It could be the face of a lost person God places on your heart with a conviction that you need to reach out to this person and reengage in your relationship with them.

Questions to ask and reflect on:

- Who do I know who is still far from Jesus whom I need to reach out to, love, and help to take a next step toward the Savior?
- What is an area of my spiritual growth I need to pay more attention to and go deeper in?
- What attitude or practice do I need to set aside so I can pay more attention to my spiritual growth journey?
- Who is a believer I know and care about who needs some encouragement to walk more closely with Jesus, and how could I be used on their growth journey?

—— Lead More (Investing in the next generation) ——

SHARING THE FOUR GENERATIONS OF DISCIPLESHIP

Identify one person you are investing in spiritually (a person you are seeking to help grow in their journey of becoming more like Jesus). It could be a family member, a friend, someone at church, or anyone you are coming alongside of to help grow in faith. In the coming week, teach them about the four generations of discipleship you are learning about in 2 Timothy 2:2. Then encourage that person to pray about and think about whom they could seek to influence in a similar way. Even if they are quite young, God can use them to help another person grow to know, love, or follow Jesus in a deeper way.

—— Love More (Sharing Jesus' love, grace, and truth) ——

DISCIPLESHIP BEFORE A PERSON FOLLOWS JESUS

Most of us have one or more people in our lives who are not yet followers of Jesus but are curious about our faith and open to hearing about our relationship with him. Evangelism and discipleship are so closely connected that we can begin the journey of discipleship while walking with a person who has not yet accepted the gift of God's grace and salvation through Jesus.

Over our decades of living lives in which discipleship and evangelism are bound together, we have discovered that two areas of spiritual growth that many nonbelievers are quite open to are prayer and service (two of the markers of maturity). Consider inviting a person you are helping to move toward Jesus into times of prayer with you and also into acts of service in partnership with you and other believers. You will be amazed at how experiences like these help move them closer to the Savior.

Bible Engagement

The Power of an Unchanging Message in an Uncertain World

The Bible is the Holy Spirit–breathed truth of heaven. Jesus is the living Word of God, and while he walked this earth, he loved the written Word. He knew it, quoted it, and let the Scriptures speak to him and through him. As his followers, we need to know the Scriptures, love them, and follow what they teach. As we do this, the world will see an unchanging message of truth in a world of radical uncertainty. God's Word will send us out on Jesus' mission and teach us how to live in the world so that Jesus' light shines brightly.

— Welcome —

The Bible is without rival the top-selling book in the history of the world. Many modern lists of bestselling books exclude the Bible because it would top the lists every month of every year. The Bible has been translated into more than seven hundred languages, and the New Testament exists in another 1,550 languages. Through the work of devoted and faithful translators, at least a portion of the Bible is now available in 1,160 more languages. This means that people from more than 3,400 language groups have access to part or all of the Bible. No other book comes close to that!

There are many excellent translations of the Hebrew, Greek, and Aramaic languages of the biblical texts. In a normal year, more than 100 million copies of the Bible are printed globally. About a quarter of those are purchased or given away in the United States. Current sales of Bibles in the United States (population just over 333 million people) would allow each person in the entire country to get a new Bible about every thirteen years.

The question is not whether the Bible is available. It is! There are even free apps that offer the Bible in an electronic format that can be read in multiple translations on a phone, tablet, or computer. The Bible has never been more readily available than it is today.

The question is whether people are growing in their engagement with the Bible. Are Christians reading or listening to the text of the Scriptures? Are we growing to love this divine book breathed by the Spirit of our God? Are we meditating on its truth, letting it shape our attitudes, and following its teachings?

Most of us own a Bible (or Bibles). The question is, do the truth and message of the Bible own us?

> ## Bible engagement and knowledge of the Scriptures should lead to transformed lives.

— Share —

What place did the Bible have in your life growing up, and what role does the Bible play in your life today?

— Watch —

Play the video for session 2 of the *Organic Disciples* small group experience. (These are free at www.OrganicDisciples.org/SmallGroupResources.) As you watch, use the following outline to record any thoughts, questions, or key points that stand out to you.

The Living Word loved the written Word.

- Scripture was in Jesus' heart and on his lips.

- Jesus prayed Scripture.

- Jesus knew the power of Scripture in spiritual battles.

So many Bibles, so little time

- Love, know, and follow.

- It is time to feast.

- Bible memorization: it's not just for Sunday-school kids.

The world needs good news.

- The world wants what Christians have.

- The Bible reveals the mission of God and then calls us to join him on that mission.

> ### If we know the Scriptures, we will hear the call to go and make disciples of all nations.

- The Bible tells us who we are.

— Discuss —

With your group, discuss what you have just watched and explore these concepts in Scripture. Use the following questions to guide your discussion.

1. When did you receive your first Bible, and what were you taught about the truth, authority, and practical nature of the Bible?

2. **Read:** Matthew 27:45–50 and Psalm 22:1. In his moment of deepest pain and anguish, Jesus cried the words of Scripture from the depths of his soul. What do you learn from the Savior's example in this account? How can you internalize Scripture so that it is in your heart and on your lips in hard times?

> Meditating on and quoting Scripture in
> the darkest of moments was the pathway
> of Jesus, and it should be ours as well.

3. **Read:** Matthew 4:1–11. In an epic spiritual battle, Jesus quoted Scripture three times, each from the book of Deuteronomy. How is the truth of the Bible the best weapon for our spiritual battles?

4. Where is spiritual warfare raging in your life (or in the life of someone you love), and how can the truth and power of the Bible help you stand strong in this battle? If a specific passage has been practical and powerful for you, feel free to share it with your group.

5. **Read:** Matthew 5:17–19 and 2 Timothy 3:14–17. Jesus and the writers of the Bible were clear about the veracity and authority of Scripture. Why is it essential that followers of Jesus believe and trust the teaching of the Bible? What are some possible consequences if our view of the Bible's truthfulness erodes?

6. **Read:** Psalm 119:97–100. What does it look like when a follower of Jesus loves the Bible? What can help us love God's written truth at a deeper level?

7. **Read:** James 1:22–25. What dangers might we face if we increase our understanding of Scripture but fail to follow what it says and apply its truth to our daily lives?

8. If we acquire knowledge of the Bible but our lives don't mirror its messages, how might that damage our witness to a nonbelieving world that is watching us closely?

> Even when it is challenging or rubs against our preferences or preconceived notions, we are called to adjust our lives to the teaching of the Bible.

9. What next step can you take to grow in your engagement with the Bible? How can your group encourage you as you take this step?

READ AND REFLECT

Each session, you will be given a key verse or verses to learn from one of the passages covered in the video teaching. This week, your suggested verses are 2 Timothy 3:16–17:

> All Scripture is God-breathed and is useful for teaching, rebuking, correcting and training in righteousness, so that the servant of God may be thoroughly equipped for every good work.
> **—2 TIMOTHY 3:16–17**

Silently or as a group, read these verses three or four times. What is their message? Consider committing these verses to memory over the next week.

RESPOND

When you think of all you have learned about Bible engagement in this session, what is one big lesson that has locked into your heart or one specific action that will impact your life?

PRAY

Close your group time by praying in any of the following directions:

- Thank God for the staggering reality that he has revealed his truth to us in the pages of the Bible and that he has preserved his message by the power of the Holy Spirit.
- Ask for the strength and discipline to study the Scriptures so that you can believe them and speak them out in your spiritual battles.
- Pray for absolute confidence in the truthfulness of God's Word, from beginning to end.
- Ask God for an ever-increasing love for his Word and for the courage and strength to follow what it teaches, even when this means being countercultural.
- Ask the Holy Spirit to show you the good news that is revealed on page after page of the Bible, and pray for opportunities to share these messages of hope with people who are longing for something better and life-giving.

The biblical narrative invites us into God's

search for the lost. The God of the Bible is

never passive. He is always on the move.

Adventures in Organic Discipleship

Session 2

Go deeper into the material you have covered in this session by engaging in the following between-session learning experiences. Each week, you will find four practical and life-impacting experiences you can engage in to go deeper as a disciple.

— Learn More (Growing your mind as a disciple) —

LEARN THE WHOLE STORY

Some years ago, we walked with our congregation through the whole story of the Bible. It took most of a year. Many of the students and adults in our church had never put together the beautiful and unified story of the Scriptures because they had not read the whole biblical story or had not understood the flow of the biblical narrative.

We used a chronologically organized collection of biblical passages and stories that are woven with some brief commentary to tie the narrative together. It is called *The Story: The Bible as One Continuing Story of God and His People*. We also partnered with our friend Randy Frazee to write a thirty-two-week small-group study that follows the reading of the biblical story and the preaching experience.

If you want to learn the epic story of the whole Bible, consider reading *The Story*. You could read it in a relatively short amount of time and gain amazing new insights into the message of the Bible. If you find it transformational in your faith, you might even want to look into walking through it with a small group or a whole church.

— Live More (Developing spiritual disciplines) —

MEMORIZE A FAMILIAR PASSAGE OF THE BIBLE

Think about a passage from the Bible you are familiar with and would like to gain deep knowledge of through memorization and reflection. It might be Psalm 23; John 3:16–17; Romans 8:37–39; Proverbs 3:5–6; or some other passage.

Write the passage reference here:

Write the passage in the space below. Don't type it, but write it out. (This helps lock the words in your mind and heart.)

Write down a few truths in this passage that strike you:

Memorize the passage. Take as much time as you need: days, weeks, or a month. Go over it many times every day. Say the words out loud. You might want to record yourself reading the passage on your phone and listen to it. You can even say the words out loud as you listen to your recording. Let the passage's truth and message fill your heart and mind.

— Lead More (Investing in the next generation) —

READING THE BIBLE IN COMMUNITY

If you have a person you are investing in spiritually and helping to grow as a disciple, agree on a book of the Bible to read together. You might read a chapter or more each day. You can each keep notes of what you are learning, how God is speaking to you, and what changes are happening in your lives. Then meet weekly face to face, on a video chat, or on the phone to share three things:

1. What you have learned.
2. How the lessons you are learning are changing your thinking, attitudes, or outlook.
3. What actions you feel the Lord wants you to take as a result of what God is teaching you through the Scriptures.

A fun note: The person you do this with will likely be a follower of Jesus, but you could also do this with a spiritually curious person. The spiritually curious are often open to studying the Bible. We once led a small-group Bible study in our neighborhood, and a number of the people who came were not yet followers of Jesus.

—— Love More (Sharing Jesus' love, grace, and truth) ——

SHARING PRACTICAL AND LIFE-CHANGING LESSONS

When we hear God's Word in a sermon, read the Bible in the community of a small group, or open the Scriptures in the quiet of our homes, our focus is often on what we feel God wants to say to us. This is great, and we should always be listening to the Scriptures for our own sakes.

But what if we added an exciting new dynamic? What if every time we read the Bible or heard it being read, we also listened with a nonbelieving person in mind? What if we were attentive to God's messages that would touch their heart, improve their life, or raise their spirits?

Try this exercise in the next week. Write down what you heard, read, or learned from the Bible and how it could impact a spiritually curious person you know and love.

The person's name:

Pause to pray. Ask God to open your eyes and ears to notice lessons, ideas, and insights that this person would resonate with.

Write down truths, insights, and inspiration you might share with this person:

- From my study of the Bible

- From a sermon I heard

- From a blog, podcast, or article I read

- From a show I watched

- From a group Bible study I attended

- From a book I read or listened to

- From a song I heard

Pray for a great moment to share one or more of these insights with this person you care about. As you share, if they seem interested, let them know where you learned this idea, that it came from the Bible. You might want to study that passage of the Bible together.

Finally, ask if they want you to pass along your source material, including the passage from the Bible; a link to a song, article, blog, or podcast; a copy of a book; a link to a sermon; or whatever might help them take the next step in their journey toward Jesus.

SESSION 3

Passionate Prayer

*How Talking with God Opens
Our Hearts to the World*

Jesus was in constant communication with his Father and prayed for his followers and for those who were wandering far from fellowship with God. As disciples, praying should be like breathing. We can live in intimate communication with the God who made us and loves us. As we grow in the spiritual marker of passionate prayer, we will find ourselves praying for and with those who still need to discover and embrace the amazing grace of Jesus.

—— Welcome ——

What if . . . God actually hears our prayers? What a staggering idea! That the King of all kings, the Lord of the universe, the creator of the heavens and the earth, the almighty God is aware of every whisper of our souls and cry of our hearts. What if, among the voices of the eight billion people who are living on the planet, God recognizes yours?

What if . . . God cares about our joys, needs, hurts, and dreams? Now take it up a notch.

What if God not only hears your voice when you call out to him, but he cares? What a thought! The one who made and sustains the heavens and all of the stars cares about your needs, struggles, and dreams. What if God's heart breaks over your loneliness and he delights when you tell him about your joy?

What if . . . God is truly powerful enough to move mountains and change things? Now we are getting somewhere! Could it be that the God who made you actually has power to heal your brokenness, fill your emptiness, strengthen you in weakness, and provide all that you need? What if God is able to take care of you and every other person who calls on his mighty name?

What if . . . God answers our prayers and acts on our requests? This is a mind-bending idea—a God who hears us, cares about us, has power to act, and then actually shows up, works in power, and answers our prayers. What if, when we pray for things that honor him and are in line with his loving will, we can see world-changing prayers answered over and over and over again?

What if . . . God does more because of prayer than we imagine or dream? Could it be that God is closer than we think, more active than we notice, and quicker to answer prayer than we have imagined?

One more.

What if . . . we prayed more and with greater confidence that God hears and is ready to answer? The answer to this question is as big as the God to whom we pray. The sky is the limit when we pray to the one and only God, who is infinite in love, power, and creativity.

So let's pray more than ever!

> **Every time you pray, you declare with confidence that God's arms are open and you are welcome in his presence.**

— Share —

Who taught you to pray, and what did they teach you about prayer? How has your understanding of prayer grown through the years?

— Watch —

Play the video for session 3 of the *Organic Disciples* small group experience. (These are free at www.OrganicDisciples.org/SmallGroupResources.) As you watch, use the following outline to record any thoughts, questions, or key points that stand out to you.

Jesus loved talking with his Father.

- Praying in the flow of life with eyes wide open

- Prayer as a priority of the soul

> When the apostle Paul wrote, "Pray continually," he was not saying we have to talk with God every second of every day. The good news is that we can talk with him at any time. God is always available.

God loves hearing from you.

- Invited into the presence of royalty

- The curtain is torn from top to bottom.

- From the heights and from the depths

Prayer changes the world.

- Praying for the world

- Praying *with* those who don't yet know Jesus
  > The when
  > The how
  > The why
- What happens when Christians pray?

— Discuss —

With your group, discuss what you have just watched and explore these concepts in Scripture. Use the following questions to guide your discussion.

1. Tell about a time God answered a prayer you lifted up to him. How did his answer to prayer impact you or someone you were praying for?

2. **Read:** Mark 1:35; Matthew 14:15–19; Mark 7:33–35; and Mark 14:32–36. Jesus prayed all through the day in a variety of situations. What are ways you can incorporate prayer into the flow of a normal day? Think in terms of silent prayer and prayers out loud. Think about prayers with your eyes closed and with your eyes wide open. Come up with ideas for prayer between you and God, and for prayer that is lifted up with other Christians you encounter during your day.

3. **Read:** Luke 6:12–16; John 11:38–44; and Luke 22:39–46. These are just a few examples of Jesus' praying before big decisions and in the big moments in his life. What do you learn from his habit of calling out to the Father in the big moments?

> Being a disciple means seeking to live like
> our Lord. Praying before, during, and after
> the big moments of life was normal behavior
> for Jesus, and it should be for us as well.

4. What is a big moment you are facing right now? How can your group be praying for you?

5. **Read:** John 17:6–19. In this passage, we hear Jesus praying for his followers. That includes you! What kinds of prayers did our Savior lift up for us? How can we adopt his way of praying for other Christians in our churches, in our communities, and around the world?
    Jesus' Prayer:How We Can Pray:

6. **Read:** 1 Thessalonians 5:17. We tend to reserve prayer for specific times and sacred places. What does it mean to become people who pray continually? Share about a surprising place or time you found yourself praying.

7. If we are not careful, we can let our prayer lives become a list of things we want. The Bible presents a rich tapestry of varied and beautiful kinds of prayer. How do each of these expressions of prayer help us move forward in our journeys of spiritual growth?

    > Prayers of *thankfulness* (telling God we are glad for all he has done)

    > Prayers of *confession* (telling God we are sorry for our sins and asking for power to live in obedience to his will and ways)

    > Prayers of *praise* (telling God what we love about his character)

    > Prayers of *lament* (telling God where we are hurting, brokenhearted, fearful, and confused while declaring our trust in him)

> Prayers for *wisdom* (asking God for insight and direction and the Holy Spirit's leading)

> *Imprecatory* prayers (expressing honest anger and even vengeful feelings to God and asking him to deal with those who have hurt us, so that we won't act on our anger)

What is one kind of prayer you need to explore more and spend more time lifting up to God?

8. **Read:** Matthew 6:5–8. Our Savior gave us a specific and powerful prayer direction for reaching out to the world with his message. What did Jesus call us to pray? Why do you think this was his focal point? What are ways we can increase our prayers for ourselves and others so that we will engage more with nonbelievers and increasingly share our faith in organic ways?

One step in growing a practice of unleashing God's presence through praying with spiritually hungry people is to believe that many of them will welcome prayer and say yes when we ask.

READ AND REFLECT

Each session, you will be given a key verse to learn from one of the passages covered in the video teaching. This week, your suggested verse is 1 Thessalonians 5:17.

> Pray continually.
> **–1 THESSALONIANS 5:17**

Silently or as a group, read this verse three or four times. What is its message? Consider committing this verse to memory over the next week.

RESPOND

When you think of all you have learned about passionate prayer in this session, what is one big lesson that has locked into your heart or one specific action that will impact your life?

Biblical faith is about connecting with

our Maker all day, every day.

PRAY

Close your group time by praying in any of the following directions:

- Thank Jesus for opening the way to communion and communication with the Father.
- Ask God to awaken you to the reality that you really can talk to him at any time and in any place, and invite the Holy Spirit to nudge you to pray more in the flow of your day.
- Pray about a big decision you are facing and invite your group to join you in crying out to God for his divine direction.
- Praise God that he loves you so much that he wants you to be completely honest in prayer about whatever you are feeling, from the heights to the depths.
- Pray for courage and boldness to ask a nonbeliever if you can pray with them the next time someone shares a deep need or great joy.
- Lift up a person in your life who does not yet know the love and grace of Jesus. Pray for their heart to open. Ask God to give you gracious and bold words. Cry out to Jesus to draw this person to himself and save them by his grace.

Some things will be accomplished only through prayer and the heavenly power it unleashes.

Adventures in Organic Discipleship

Go deeper into the material you have covered in this session by engaging in the following between-session learning experiences. Each week, you will find four practical and life-impacting experiences you can engage in to go deeper as a disciple.

—— Learn More (Growing your mind as a disciple) ——

LEARNING FROM THE MASTER

In the coming week, study two of the big prayers of Jesus.

Read Matthew 6:9–13. Write down insights in response to these questions:

- What kinds of things should I pray about?

- What is the heartbeat of prayer?

- What does Jesus believe about prayer?

Read John 17:1–26. Write down insights in response to these questions:

- What kinds of things should I pray about?

- What is the heartbeat of prayer?

- What does Jesus believe about prayer?

> The great Evangelist and Shepherd of the sheep prays for us as he sends us into the world. He compares our being sent to how the Father sent his Son into the world. That is a high calling!

— Live More (Developing spiritual disciplines) —

TRY KEEPING A PRAYER JOURNAL

You can do one or more of these simple exercises with pen and paper in a journal, or you can create an electronic journal on your phone, tablet, or computer. If you keep an e-journal, consider putting your device in airplane mode while you journal so you don't get distracted.

- **Idea:** Write down three single-sentence prayers of thanks for things God did the previous day and for the ways he provided, protected, showed his grace, or anything else you are thankful for.
- **Idea:** Read a portion of Scripture and write a prayer out of whatever you learned by reading God's Word.
- **Idea:** Write down a list of people you long to meet Jesus, receive his grace and friendship, and follow him as the leader of their lives. Pray for each person daily, and write down ways you believe God wants you to share his love and truth with them.

- **Idea:** Write down names of God found in the Bible and a brief prayer praising him for what each name reveals about his character.
- **Idea:** Make a list of three to four needs in your life and another list of three to four needs in the lives of people you love. Pray through this list regularly and add needs or praises as you feel led.

—— Lead More (Investing in the next generation) ——

SHARE ONE LESSON AND ONE PRAYER STORY

Share one big lesson—either written down or recorded in a short video on your phone—that God has taught you about prayer through your time as a follower of Jesus. Also, tell one story of how God has answered a prayer in your life.

Send this video or written story to one or more Christians whom God is allowing you to influence to grow closer to Jesus. Let them know you would love to talk more about why we pray and how God answers our prayers. You might even want to ask them to share one lesson they have learned about prayer and one story of answered prayer in their lives.

—— Love More (Sharing Jesus' love, grace, and truth) ——

A TESTIMONY AND AN OPEN DOOR

This will take a bold spirit, so pray first!

Consider making a short video of yourself telling a story of answered prayer. If you don't want to make a video, you can write a letter or send an email sharing your story. Send it to one spiritually curious person God has placed in your life. Let them know that you would love to talk with them about why you believe God really hears and answers prayer.

Pray that God uses this story to open the door to some rich and powerful conversations with this person.

SESSION 4

Wholehearted Worship

How Praise, Celebration, and Worship Propel Us Outward and Draw the World In

Our God is worthy of worship! Disciples delight in giving praise, glory, and honor to the only one who deserves it. When we grow in faith, worship flows from our hearts and lips. Every experience can be a time for worshiping in Spirit and in truth. When people see Christians who celebrate the goodness of God, overflow with joy, and walk in humble surrender, they become curious. When groups of believers gather and celebrate with overflowing joy and passion, the world wants to know more, and we can tell our story.

— Welcome —

Eight to ten times a year, we invite people at our worship services to respond publicly to the gospel and enter a lifesaving relationship with Jesus by placing their faith in him and committing to follow him as the leader of their lives. We do this only in worship services in which the gospel has been proclaimed with clarity. We also invite people to meet with a team to learn about the next steps of spiritual growth. Or we connect them to the resources they need to begin a healthy and growing relationship with Jesus.

What is exciting is that in more than a hundred weekends of worship services that we have made this invitation, there have been only a few times when people have not opened their hearts, cried out to God, and begun a life-changing relationship with the Savior.

The fact that people respond almost every time we invite them to receive the eternity-transforming hope of Jesus should tell us something: there are nonbelievers sitting in our church pews. The truth is, on a normal weekend, we are confident that there are a lot of spiritually curious people who have not yet embraced the Good News.

The real question is what are these people doing in a church service? Why are non-believers coming to a worship experience where the Bible is taught, songs of praise are sung, offerings are given, prayers are lifted up, and Christian fellowship is in high gear? Why do people come to our worship services week after week even though they have not yet recognized that Jesus loves them and died to set them free from their sin?

There may be many answers to this question. But one thing is certain. Worship of the living God is life changing! When God's people gather, the Holy Spirit is present in life-changing ways. And some of the greatest longings of the human heart, including the hearts of nonbelievers, are satisfied when people worship God.

We all hunger for community: community happens in worship. We long for a sense of the transcendent and an awareness that there is something bigger than us: worship satisfies this longing because God is powerfully present when his people worship. In a world of relativism, people (sometimes secretly) are looking for anything secure and unchanging: an encounter with the immutable God offers that. Human beings are made for worship, and when they find the true source of this longing and encounter the one true God who deserves their praise, something happens in their souls.

Worship is for believers in Jesus, no doubt. But worship is also for those who are seeking after God but still have not found him. Being among God's people as they worship their Lord in the Spirit and in truth might be just the thing that draws a lost person home and into the arms of Jesus.

When we slow down, open our eyes, pay attention, and take note of God's presence, we will be drawn to deeper worship.

—— Share ——

Tell about one of your first memories of being in a church worship service.

—— Watch ——

Play the video for session 4 of the *Organic Disciples* small group experience. (These are free at www.OrganicDisciples.org/SmallGroupResources.) As you watch, use the following outline to record any thoughts, questions, or key points that stand out to you.

Worthy of worship

- Jesus calls us to a lifestyle of worship.

- All of life can become worship.

Worship as a lifestyle

- Sing, praise, and celebrate.

- Worship as surrender

- Worship only God.

- The wonder of gathered worship

> True worship is about a life surrendered to
> the Father, who made us and loves us.

The world loves a good party.

- Worship invites the Holy Spirit to come in power.

- The witness of joy

- When the Spirit is in the house

- Invite spiritually curious people to gathered worship experiences.

—— Discuss ——

With your group, discuss what you have just watched and explore these concepts in Scripture. Use the following questions to guide your discussion.

1. Tell about a time when you had a sense of God's presence during a time of worship.

2. What sorts of things propel you into a place of worship? What gets in the way of your engaging deeply in worship?

3. **Read:** Mark 11:9–10; Mark 15:39; Luke 24:52; and John 1:49. When Jesus walked on this earth, people commonly responded to him by worshiping him. What are some of the ways people expressed worship toward Jesus? How did he respond to these offerings of praise and devotion?

4. **Read:** Mark 11:15–17; Luke 4:5–8; and John 4:19–25. Jesus taught his followers to be people committed to worship. What are some of the lessons Jesus shared with those who wanted to grow as worshipers?

> As his disciples, this should be our deepest
> desire: to know the Father's will and
> obey it. This is our act of worship.

5. Sometimes we limit our understanding of worship to a set time and place: in a church building for an hour on Sunday. Worship is bigger and far more beautiful. What are some of the different ways we can worship God in the normal flow of a week?

6. Tell about a time you encountered God and responded in worship when you were not in a church building.

> Whenever we seek to bring glory to God, to lift up his name and honor him, we are engaging in worship.

7. What is one way you can infuse your life with worship between the times you gather with God's people for a worship service? How can your group pray for you and cheer you on as you seek to live as a worshiper all week long?

8. How can we turn our homes into places of worship? As we invite into our homes people who are not yet Jesus followers, how can our homes be places where they experience the presence of God alive and at work?

READ AND REFLECT

Each session, you will be given a key verse to learn from one of the passages covered in the video teaching. This week, your suggested verse is John 4:23:

> "Yet a time is coming and has now come when the true worshipers will worship the Father in the Spirit and in truth, for they are the kind of worshipers the Father seeks."
> —JOHN 4:23

Silently or as a group, read this verse three or four times. What is its message? Consider committing this verse to memory over the next week.

RESPOND

When you think of all you have learned about wholehearted worship in this session, what is one big lesson that has locked into your heart or one specific action that will impact your life?

PRAY

Close your group time by praying in any of the following directions:

- Lift up prayers of worship, praise, and celebration for who God is and what he has done.
- Ask the Holy Spirit to show you anything or anyone that is taking too high of a place in your heart, and pray for courage to keep God and only God on the throne of your life.
- Ask God to help you worship him from the moment you wake until you go to sleep at night. Pray that worship becomes a consuming passion and the normal condition of your heart.
- If you are part of a church, pray that you will all grow as a worshiping community that loves Jesus and follows him in unity. If you are not faithfully and consistently engaged as a member of a worshiping community, pray for a humble heart to find a church home and become an active part of the family of God.
- Pray for a friend or family member you care about who is not yet a believer in Jesus. Ask God to give you wisdom and good timing as you look for ways to invite this person to a gathered worship experience where they will sense the presence of the Spirit and see God's people engaged in authentic worship.

Jesus lived a life of sacrifice, surrender, and alignment with the will of his Father, and that is the pattern for his followers as well.

Adventures in Organic Discipleship

Go deeper into the material you have covered in this session by engaging in the following between-session learning experiences. Each week, you will find four practical and life-impacting experiences you can engage in to go deeper as a disciple.

— Learn More (Growing your mind as a disciple) —

JESUS' TUTORIAL ON WORSHIP

Read: John 4:1–42. Prayerfully reflect on Jesus' encounter with the woman at the well. At the center of their conversation is worship. Write down your thoughts and insights below.

What does this woman seem to believe about worship?

What does Jesus believe and teach her?

How can this teaching shape the way you view worship and the way you engage as a worshiper in corporate gatherings and in the flow of your life?

True worship is never about us. God is the center of worship, or it is not truly worship.

—— Live More (Developing spiritual disciplines) ——

TAKE A WALK WITH JESUS

Take a twenty- to thirty-minute walk to be alone with Jesus. As you walk, lift up this simple prayer: "Lord Jesus Christ, teach me to worship you in Spirit and in truth."

Each time you pray these words, reflect on what it means to worship in the Spirit, what it means to worship in truth, and what it means for you to be a worshiper. Then pray this simple prayer again, reflect, and wait on the Lord.

When you are done with your walk, write down anything you feel the Lord has brought to your heart and mind.

How can I worship in the Spirit in deeper ways?

How can I worship in the truth in deeper ways?

How can I grow as a worshiper?

—— Lead More (Investing in the next generation) ——

WORSHIP AS A FAMILY

Many churches, including the one we serve, offer age-appropriate learning and worship experiences. Children go to Sunday school or kids' worship. Teens have youth classes or youth worship. This is great. But if we never worship in a gathered setting with our own children, our nieces and nephews, and our friends' children, we are missing something. Consider attending your church worship services with the whole family on occasion. Maybe once every couple of months declare a family worship time and have the younger generation come to the service you attend. Afterward talk about the elements of the worship service, what they mean, and how they help you encounter God in his beauty and glory.

As a bonus, you might talk with your pastor about planning a few multigenerational worship services a year and even canceling children's programing those weeks if it conflicts with the worship service times.

—— Love More (Sharing Jesus' love, grace, and truth) ——

SHARE A SONG

You can find a growing number of great worship songs on YouTube. If you find a song that really moves your heart and leads you to worship, pray about sharing the link to this song with a person you care about who does not yet have a relationship with Jesus.

Of course, think through the message and theology of the song. If it is biblical and honoring to Jesus, consider sending it to a friend and even share a bit about what it means to you and why you enjoy it so much. We have known a number of friends and family members who were not believers but loved music. As we shared praise songs with them, they began to enjoy worship music before they embraced the Lord who is worthy of their worship. Worship can be an avenue God uses to lead a person to faith.

SESSION 5

Humble Service

How Caring Hearts and Compassionate
Hands Show God's Love for All People

Jesus left the glory of heaven and came to serve us. His disciples joyfully serve their Savior, his church, and the world he loves. When we care like Jesus does, the world sees a vision of the servant Savior and is willing to hear our stories of who Jesus is and how he loves.

—— Welcome ——

He was an ordinary guy with a common name, Bob. In the late 1940s until the end of the Chinese Civil War, he worked with Youth for Christ and was part of a number of evangelistic rallies in China. While there, Bob was deeply moved by the devastation of homes, schools, infrastructure, and lives. Before he left for the States, he began a monthly practice of sending five dollars to a needy child back in China.

Bob decided to start an organization to help children in some of the neediest places in the world. He wanted to connect caring sponsors with struggling kids and facilitate their giving monthly support to provide food, medical care, basic physical needs, and access to the gospel. In 1950, Bob launched a small ministry he called World Vision.

In 1970, Bob felt it was time to begin another ministry to help children in desolate situations and bring them physical care and the love of Jesus. He began Samaritan's Purse. This ministry serves communities and needy people with disaster relief, surgeries for children born with heart defects, water projects, medical missionaries, and Operation Christmas Child (a Christmas box with practical and fun gifts and also a booklet with stories including the message of Christmas). The ministry also has a twelve-week follow-up discipleship and evangelism program for anyone who wants to participate.

If you ever wonder whether humble service can open the door for sharing the good news of Jesus, just remember the story of Robert (Bob) Pierce's life. Because he served in the name of Jesus, more than 124 million children have received Christmas gifts and heard the story of God's Son who was born in a manger. Between three and four million children are sponsored annually and receive care for their physical and spiritual needs. More lives have been touched than Bob could have dreamed when he started serving a needy child in China as a young man.

Compassion, mercy, service, and humble hearts can change the world and open the door to sharing Jesus' lifesaving message.

> In a dark world, humble service is a beacon
> that reveals the presence of Jesus and draws
> lost people to the heart of the Savior.

— Share —

Tell about a Christian you know who is an example of humble service. How do you see Jesus in this person, and how is their service a witness to God's love?

— Watch —

Play the video for session 5 of the *Organic Disciples* small group experience. (These are free at www.OrganicDisciples.org/SmallGroupResources.) As you watch, use the following outline to record any thoughts, questions, or key points that stand out to you.

When God knelt at our feet

- The shocking, staggering servant life of Jesus

- The world-transforming death and resurrection of Jesus

- He is still serving today.

Humility and service are radically countercultural.

- Service is not a suggestion.

- Notice the need.

- Carry the cross.

Actions that show Jesus open the door for us to speak of the Savior.

- Good deeds open doors.

- The million-dollar question, "Why?"

- Where should we serve?

> The more self-centered our world grows,
> the more our humble service will stand
> out as unusual and countercultural.

— Discuss —

With your group, discuss what you have just watched and explore these concepts in Scripture. Use the following questions to guide your discussion.

1. Jesus began serving us before he was born. His incarnation presents an awe-inspiring picture of humble service. **Read:** John 1:14 and Philippians 2:5–8. What did Jesus give up, and how did he serve us by leaving heaven and coming as one of us?

2. **Read:** John 13:1–17 and Mark 10:45. What do you learn about Jesus in these passages? What do you learn about the followers of Jesus (including yourself) as you read John 13?

3. As you think about these passages and reflect on Jesus' sacrifice on the cross, what is the connection between humble service and the gospel's coming to the world? How would the message of our faith be different if Jesus had not been incarnated, washed feet, and humbly given his life?

4. Jesus made it clear that his service is an example for us to follow. In what ways are you seeking to serve others with a humble heart? What seems to get in the way of your living self-sacrificially?

5. What is the next step you feel called to make in your journey of spiritual growth in the area of humble service? Be specific. Whom do you need to serve more, and how can you live out a plan to serve them? How can your group pray for you and challenge you to keep growing in this area?

6. **Read:** Matthew 5:13–16. Why is it important for churches and Christians to find ways to share Jesus while they are serving people in their communities? If we offer kind deeds but never point to Jesus or share his story, what might people miss?

7. What are some practical ways we can serve with humility in any of the following places?

> Where we work

> Where we go to school

> Where we live

> Where we play

> Where we shop

> Some other place we go regularly

Now look back at the "where" you can serve and talk about how you might naturally share the message, story, and good news of Jesus while you are serving.

8. What are some ways your small group could be part of a service project in your community that shows the love of Jesus and shares the good news of the Savior? Consider picking one of these ideas and partner together to grow in humble service as a community.

Humble service is not the end of evangelism, it is the door that opens the way to speak words of life, tell Jesus' story, and share the good news of the hope that is found in him alone.

READ AND REFLECT

Each session, you will be given a key verse to learn from one of the passages covered in the video teaching. This week, your suggested verse is Mark 10:45:

> "For even the Son of Man did not come to be served, but to serve, and to give his life as a ransom for many."
> —MARK 10:45

Silently or as a group, read this verse three or four times. What is its message? Consider committing this verse to memory over the next week.

RESPOND

When you think of all you have learned about humble service in this session, what is one big lesson that has locked into your heart or one specific action that will impact your life?

PRAY

Close your group time by praying in any of the following directions:

- Lift up praise to Jesus for humbly entering our world, caring for those who hurt, washing feet, and offering his life for us.
- Ask God to increase your awareness of needs around you so that you can slow down and offer acts of service in the spirit and name of Jesus.
- Invite the Holy Spirit to search your heart and help you identify those places and situations where you tend to drop your guard and shift into self-serving attitudes and actions.
- Thank God for the people who have served you like Jesus did, and praise God for their example and their lives of faithful and humble service.

- Ask God to make the place where you live a hub of service in your neighborhood. Pray for Jesus' light to shine from the place you live to the people around you.
- Pray that your acts of service will reveal Jesus' presence and open the door for spiritual conversations with people who are not yet following the Savior.

Humble service demands that we decrease our pace and increase our attentiveness. God provides daily opportunities for us to stop, care, help, and bless people through small and large acts of service.

Adventures in Organic Discipleship

Session 5

Go deeper into the material you have covered in this session by engaging in the following between-session learning experiences. Each week, you will find four practical and life-impacting experiences you can engage in to go deeper as a disciple.

—— Learn More (Growing your mind as a disciple) ——

STUDY THE EXAMPLE OF FOOT WASHING

Read: John 13:1–17. Reflect on the following questions:

What did Jesus know about himself before and while he was washing feet?

Who was at the table with Jesus, and why did Jesus wash everyone's feet?

What was Jesus' attitude as he served his followers?

What key lessons did Jesus teach after washing his followers' feet?

What truth is God teaching you through this passage?

— Live More (Developing spiritual disciplines) —

WASH A FOOT A DAY (OR MAYBE A PAIR OF FEET)

For one week, do all you can to offer a large or small act of unexpected service to one person who does not yet follow Jesus. Keep a short journal for the week.

If any of these people ask you why you served them as you did, be ready to share what you are learning about Jesus as a humble servant and his call for you to follow his example. If they ask more questions, talk about how Jesus has served you with his life and how he wants to serve them as well.

DAY 1

Act of service

How the person responded

What happened in my heart as I served

DAY 2

Act of service

How the person responded

What happened in my heart as I served

Act of service

How the person responded

What happened in my heart as I served

Act of service

How the person responded

What happened in my heart as I served

DAY 5

Act of service

How the person responded

What happened in my heart as I served

DAY 6

Act of service

How the person responded

What happened in my heart as I served

Act of service

How the person responded

What happened in my heart as I served

> As we give with generous and joy-filled
> hearts, the world can see a picture of God's
> love. Joyful generosity captures the attention
> of a world possessed by possessions.

—— Lead More (Investing in the next generation) ——
SERVE JESUS IN COMMUNITY

In your group time, you identified a number of service projects you could do together. Hopefully you chose one and set a time to serve as a group. Now think back on the options you discussed and pick one to do with a person you are helping to grow in their faith and go deeper as a disciple. Invite that person to join you. Read John 13:1–17 together before you serve, and pray that God will use you to extend his care and give you an opportunity to have a conversation about Jesus.

— Love More (Sharing Jesus' love, grace, and truth) —

SERVE TOGETHER

If you are engaged in a service ministry through your church or in your community, invite a spiritually searching friend to join you. If they say yes, look for an opportunity to share the story of John 13 with them, and explain how Jesus loved to serve others and that you are seeking to become more like him. You might even ask if you can pray for both of you as you prepare to serve together. Ask Jesus to guide your hands and hearts and for his love to be felt as you serve.

SESSION 6

Joyful Generosity

How Sharing Our Time, Resources, and Abilities Captures the Attention of the World

Jesus gave all he had and all he was for us. With divine generosity, he left glory, came to earth, took our sins, and died in our place. Now he calls his disciples to walk in his footsteps. As we give with generous and joy-filled hearts, the world can see a picture of God's love. Joyful generosity captures the attention of a world possessed by possessions.

—— Welcome ——

Keith and Linda were an amazing generous couple. When we came to serve in the small struggling church they attended, we were immediately drawn to them. They loved freely. Both of them served in the church and offered leadership and help anywhere there was a need. They always seemed to have words of encouragement and helpful challenge on their lips. When there was a monetary need, they quietly made a difference in others' lives. Put simply, they looked a lot like Jesus. They were joyfully generous.

As we got to know Keith and Linda over the years, their example shaped our lives. Being around them when we were young people in Christian service inspired us to view giving as an honor and a privilege. They seemed to love investing their lives, time, abilities, and resources in people and in the things that last forever.

When we were in seminary (we both earned our master's degrees while serving at their church), Keith decided to audit a seminary class. Although he owned a successful business, he also had a passion for theology and a dream to go into full-time Christian service someday. It was on one of our drives together to our seminary class that Keith shared some things that stretched our faith and expanded our understanding of joyful generosity.

"Hey, Keith, you are so naturally generous. Do you see tithing [giving the first ten percent of what you earn to God's work] as your guideline for giving?" He smiled and said, "No way! If I tithed, I would be out of God's will!" There was an awkward pause, and then he explained. With humble honesty, he said, "Years ago Linda and I had a clear conviction that we needed to devote the first fifty percent of all God gives us back to the work of Jesus. If we gave only ten percent, we would be way out of line!" It took a few moments for us to compute that idea. It seemed reckless and over the top. But when we looked at the rich and joy-filled lives Keith and Linda were experiencing, it made sense.

Eventually, they sold their business and used the money to live on while Keith went back to school. Some years later, he began to serve as a pastor of a wonderful church out toward the East Coast. We can say with confidence that the congregation they served was blessed to follow a couple who lived with a generosity that revealed the presence, grace, and joy of Jesus.

— Share —

Tell about a Christian you know who lives with authentic and joyful generosity. What do they share, and how does their lifestyle reveal Jesus' presence and goodness?

As disciples of Jesus who want to be like him in every way, we should invite the Holy Spirit to give us a new and deeper vision of what the Son of God did when he left the glory of heaven and entered our world, becoming Jesus of Nazareth, the Jewish Messiah and savior of the world.

— Watch —

Play the video for session 6 of the *Organic Disciples* small group experience. (These are free at www.OrganicDisciples.org/SmallGroupResources.) As you watch, use the following outline to record any thoughts, questions, or key points that stand out to you.

Jesus gave it all!

- What Jesus gave for you and me

- Generosity was a lifestyle for Jesus.

> When he gave himself for us, the boundless
> one was placed in the confines of a virgin
> womb—infinite being in a human embryo, the
> omnipresent Lord bound in human flesh.

The adventure of a generous life

- We all have a family history and a personal background that influence us.

- Generosity goes against the current.

- How do I grow in joyful generosity?

The world will see Jesus' presence when we are generous in his name.

- If you want to get the attention of the world, be generous—no strings attached!

- How does a joyfully generous life open the door for the gospel?

Every time a follower of Jesus is generous in our selfish world, we show the heart of our God. If people are stunned or surprised by someone who gives with contagious joy, it opens the door for spiritual conversations.

— Discuss —

With your group, discuss what you have just watched and explore these concepts in Scripture. Use the following questions to guide your discussion.

1. When Jesus came as a baby, lived on this earth, and died for our sins, what were some of the ways he displayed a generous heart and life?

2. How have you experienced Jesus' generosity toward you?

> No Christian would question whether our Lord Jesus is the most generous being in the universe. What he gave up for us is beyond our wildest imagination. If we had a thousand lifetimes to serve Jesus, we could not begin to pay back what he gave when he emptied himself and took on flesh.

3. **Read:** Hebrews 12:1–3. What do you think the writer of Hebrews means by these words about Jesus: "For the joy set before him he endured the cross" (v. 2)? How can generosity to the point of death bring joy?

4. **Read:** Luke 19:1–10. How did Jesus' presence and power transform Zacchaeus's life? How did his view of material things change when he received Jesus' generous love?

5. **Read:** Luke 12:13–21 and Matthew 6:24. Jesus gave some clear warnings about hoarding and being possessed by possessions. What is Jesus' warning? Why do you think he wants us to be careful about wealth and the accumulation of stuff?

6. **Read:** Malachi 3:8–12 and Luke 6:38. When God promises blessing in response to our generosity, it means far more than just dollars and cents (though God can bless this way when he chooses to). What are some of the different kinds of blessings a person might receive when they grow in joyful generosity? Tell about a blessing you received from God that was not monetary.

7. Read the following list and identify one way you can grow in joyful generosity. Tell about a step you believe you need to take to increase your commitment to sharing the material things God has given you:
   > Commit to set aside a specific percentage of your income on a weekly or monthly basis and give it to the work of Jesus at the church you are part of.
   > Pay attention to God's prompting to find one spontaneous opportunity to help a person in need by sharing food, clothes, money, or a gift card. Be creative.
   > Search your heart and honestly assess whether money has become an idol for you.
   > Do something with family or friends that helps you celebrate and enjoy what God has given, and make part of this experience talking about God's amazing provision.

> Give away something that just seems to be taking up space and you don't really enjoy very often. Give it to a person who would delight in it, or sell it and give the money to a good Christian ministry or cause.

If you start giving things away, don't make it an excuse to get new stuff.

8. Why does the life of a joyfully generous Christian catch the attention of non-believers who are spiritually curious?

Tell about a time you saw the life of a consistently generous Christian open the door for them to share Jesus' love, grace, and goodness with others.

How can your group pray for you as you grow more generous for the sake of Jesus?

READ AND REFLECT

Each session, you will be given a key verse or verses to learn from one of the passages covered in the video teaching. This week, your suggested verses are Hebrews 12:1–2:

> Therefore, since we are surrounded by such a great cloud of witnesses, let us throw off everything that hinders and the sin that so easily entangles. And let us run with perseverance the race marked out for us, fixing our eyes on Jesus, the pioneer and perfecter of faith. For the joy set before him he endured the cross, scorning its shame, and sat down at the right hand of the throne of God.
>
> —HEBREWS 12:1-2

Silently or as a group, read these verses three or four times. What is their message? Consider committing these verses to memory over the next week.

RESPOND

When you think of all you have learned about joyful generosity in this session, what is one big lesson that has locked into your heart or one specific action that will impact your life?

PRAY

Close your group time by praying in any of the following directions:

- Thank the Father for the generous gift of his only Son, Jesus.
- Praise Jesus for all he gave up so that he could offer us salvation.
- Ask God to increase your generosity to the point that you take delight in being lavish toward others.
- Invite the Holy Spirit to show you whether material things have become an idol for you. Lay them at Jesus' feet and surrender them to the Lord who gives you every perfect gift.
- Ask God to help you see all you have as gifts from him, and pray for courage to live with open hands and an open heart to share what he has placed in your care.
- Pray that you will increase in generosity and that your example will open the door to many conversations with nonbelievers about God's faithfulness, provision, and love.

If we live free from the entanglements of possessions,

people will want what we have. Then we can tell

them about the one who has satisfied our souls,

provided for our needs, and given us inheritances

in heaven that can never be taken away.

Adventures in Organic Discipleship

Session 6

Go deeper into the material you have covered in this session by engaging in the following between-session learning experiences. Each week, you will find four practical and life-impacting experiences you can engage in to go deeper as a disciple.

—— Learn More (Growing your mind as a disciple) ——

GET SATISFIED

A close friend of ours, Jeff Manion, wrote a powerful book about contentment and a biblical view on how we relate to the stuff of this world. It is titled *Satisfied: Discovering Contentment in a World of Consumption*. It can be read over a few weeks in a devotional and reflective way. If you want to grow your mind on this topic and increase your joy, freedom, and generosity, reading this book will help and inspire you.

— Live More (Developing spiritual disciplines) —

READ, REFLECT, AND MEDITATE

Every day for a week, read the following passage three or four times. Read prayerfully. Read slowly. Reflect on each idea and exhortation. Let the themes turn over in your mind and heart through the day. Then do it again the next day. Keep a simple list of the lessons you sense God is speaking to your heart.

> But godliness with contentment is great gain. For we brought nothing into the world, and we can take nothing out of it. But if we have food and clothing, we will be content with that. Those who want to get rich fall into temptation and a trap and into many foolish and harmful desires that plunge people into ruin and destruction. For the love of money is a root of all kinds of evil. Some people, eager for money, have wandered from the faith and pierced themselves with many griefs. But you, man of God, flee from all this, and pursue righteousness, godliness, faith, love, endurance and gentleness. Fight the good fight of the faith.
>
> **—1 TIMOTHY 6:6–12**

Insights from Day 1

Insights from Day 2

Insights from Day 3

Insights from Day 4

Insights from Day 5

Insights from Day 6

Insights from Day 7

— Lead More (Investing in the next generation) —

TALK ABOUT TREASURES

With one or more of the people you are seeking to help grow in their faith, talk about the connection of our hearts to what we truly treasure (Matt. 6:21). You might want to use a couple of these questions to get the conversation started:

- If you look back over a normal week, where do you invest most of your time and money? What does this say about where your heart is?
- Of all the things you use your money for or invest your money in, what gets you most excited, and why do you think this is the case?
- If you received an unexpected inheritance of $10,000, how do you think you would use this gift?

> Even people who do not follow Jesus or acknowledge him as Savior have the sense that Jesus was good, kind, gracious, and generous. They expect people who bear the name of Christ to be like the one they claim to follow.

— Love More (Sharing Jesus' love, grace, and truth) —

BE PREPARED WITH AN ANSWER

If a nonbelieving person in your life asked you why you are so generous and what makes you so willing to share with others, what would you say?

Write down a couple of responses that speak of God's goodness to you and your desire to be generous like Jesus. Put these responses in words that a friend or family member would clearly understand.

I could say:

I could say:

I could say:

Consistent Community

The Power of Togetherness in a Polarized World

God exists in eternal, perfect trinitarian community. Jesus made relationships a priority when he walked this earth, and he called his disciples to live in consistent loving community. When we walk in loving fellowship with God and each other, people will see that we have what their hearts long for. This kind of community draws people toward the only one who can heal their hearts, bind their wounds, and satisfy their hunger to belong.

— Welcome —

After a two-week ministry trip to the Netherlands with a team from our church that included all three of our young sons, we took a few days to see the sights in London. One afternoon, we stood outside the tall gates of Buckingham Palace near a beautiful fountain and watched as hundreds of guests waited in a line that stretched for a number of blocks and then turned a corner. Each woman was dressed in her most elegant gown and wore an elaborate hat. The men were all in formal attire with coats and ties, and many wore top hats. It was a spectacle!

We asked some locals and found out the queen was having a tea. Her guests waited with polite enthusiasm in the warm afternoon air. You could sense their pride and excitement. They were invited in one or two at a time as the others stood in patient expectation of their turn.

Given the volume of people waiting to see her, it was clear that the queen was not sitting around having long conversations with close friends over tea. This was a formal event. Although we stayed outside (apparently our invitation had been lost in the mail), we could imagine how each person would be escorted into the queen's presence, pass by Her Majesty, bow or curtsy, and then move out to another location where they would have a cup of tea and mingle with other guests.

You can be certain no one said, "How you doin', Lizzy?" or, "How's it going, Alexandra Mary?" or, "Thanks for the invite, Elizabeth!" There is no chance anyone jumped past security and gave the queen a bear hug. Not one person standing in line to "have tea" with Her Royal Majesty would have addressed her informally. There is strict protocol at these kinds of events. Yes, they were invited to tea, but they did not experience community with their queen. They came as her subjects and left feeling honored to have been invited but having come no closer to the monarch.

Jesus was and is the King of Kings, the Lord of Glory, the maker of heaven and earth, the Son of God, and the savior of the world. Yet he calls us friends. Jesus shared meals with both the powerful and the outcast. He conversed with both his closest friends and strangers on the street. He touched the sick, and they reached out and touched him too. Our King left a heavenly throne and a place of majesty that would make Buckingham Palace look modest. He lived among the people he loved. Community was his passion and intimacy his practice.

In a world where so many people feel left out or ostracized, the call to consistent community is a source of hope and healing. The God who exists in the eternal community of trinitarian harmony not only models the beauty of relational intimacy, he invites us to come near. When Jesus died on the cross, the curtain in the temple was torn in two by the divine hands of God to show us that we are invited into the most holy place—his presence—anytime! What a timely message for our broken world. Jesus, the

King of Glory, invites you to come near. He loves community. No need to wear a fancy hat or your best outfit. You don't have to wait in line. Hey, you don't even need an invitation—he already gave it. Just come on over. His door, arms, and heart are always open.

—— Share ——

Tell a story about being invited in and feeling warmly welcomed, or share about a time when you felt excluded or pushed out of a social situation. Why are these moments so locked into our memory banks and hearts?

—— Watch ——

Play the video for session 7 of the *Organic Disciples* small group experience. (These are free at www.OrganicDisciples.org/SmallGroupResources.) As you watch, use the following outline to record any thoughts, questions, or key points that stand out to you.

God needed nothing but invited us to be his friends.

- God's nature

- Jesus loves people—ordinary folks like you and me.

- Jesus understood the pain of broken relationships.

Jesus called the disciples to be with him and share life in all of its glory and pain. He invited his followers to experience the pedestrian and sublime. The disciples walked in Jesus' steps, and they could see every footprint he left.

Why we are better together

- We were created for community and are hardwired for fellowship.

- The complexity of community

- Committing to consistent community

All through the Scriptures, we learn that God accomplishes more for his glory through his people together than if they are disconnected.

> **The way we love people shows the world that Jesus is present and active.**

- The magnetic power of Spirit-infused community

- The power of an inviting and loving church

- What the world sees when we live in consistent community

— Discuss —

With your group, discuss what you have just watched and explore these concepts in Scripture. Use the following questions to guide your discussion.

1. What are some of the signs you notice in the lives of people around you that show their need for connection and community?

2. When a church is healthy and functioning as our Lord intends, we will love God, care for each other, and embrace people who have not yet accepted Jesus' offer of grace. We will be a loving and accepting community. When that is a congregation's reality, what do we have to offer to fulfill the deepest longings of people's hearts? What will help your church take a good step in this direction?

> The closer we walk with Jesus, the more
> our hearts will break for the lost, and
> the more our lives will orient toward
> those who are still wandering.

3. **Read:** Matthew 4:18–22. What did the call to follow Jesus mean for his first disciples? The focal point of Jesus' call was to "follow him" and be with him. What should following Jesus and being with him look like in our lives today?

4. Jesus loved community, and he mixed with, mingled with, served, and loved people from every walk of life. Who were some of the people Jesus connected with and had community with when he walked this earth? (Open your Bible or Bible app and scroll through the Gospels.) Why do you think Jesus lived in community with such an eclectic group of people? What can his followers today learn from this example?

5. **Read:** Genesis 1:26–28 and Romans 12:3–8. In his creation of humanity and in his creation of the church, God made it clear that we are made for community and connection with each other and with him. Why do you think God hardwired us for community? Why do so many people resist his call to live in community?

6. **Read:** Mark 12:29–31. What did Jesus say are the two most important things his followers should do with their time and their lives? Share one practical way you need to grow in loving community with God, and one way you feel the Lord wants you to grow in community with your neighbors.

7. Jesus spent a lot of time around tables, a place of intimate community. How can sharing meals with groups of believers grow your connectedness and unity? How can inviting spiritually curious people around a table for food, conversation, laughter, and sharing life open the door for them to experience Jesus' presence? How can your group pray for you as you look for an opportunity to gather around a table with someone in your life who is still finding their way toward Jesus?

> Table fellowship creates a place to move from casual chatting to deep conversation. If disciples of Jesus are to live as he did, we need to spend more time around tables sharing food and life.

8. Think about the church you attend. When you gather, what do you do to make a nonbelieving visitor feel welcome, loved, and a part of your community? How can you enhance these things? What do you do that might make these same people feel unwelcome or excluded? How can you reduce these things? (Note: if what makes someone feel uncomfortable is the truth of the gospel or the teaching of the Scriptures, we never compromise on these.)

9. God expects some things to be common and normative when his people gather in community. Talk about a few of these things and identify ways you can increase these features of your Christian community.

Our Community Should
> Reveal *love* in action
> Be an example of real and deep *forgiveness*
> Look as *diverse* as the place God has planted us in and also be an example of *unity*
> *Serve* as a group and everywhere God sends us
> Be filled with a palpable sense of the *Holy Spirit's presence*

How can you help increase one or more of these in the life of your church?

Church services, small groups of believers, loving Christian families, Jesus-centered friendships, and discipling relationships are all incubators that God uses to help us grow in faith.

READ AND REFLECT

Each session, you will be given a key verse or verses to learn from one of the passages covered in the video teaching. This week, your suggested verses are Romans 12:4–5:

> For just as each of us has one body with many members, and these members do not all have the same function, so in Christ we, though many, form one body, and each member belongs to all the others.
>
> **—ROMANS 12:4–5**

Silently or as a group, read these verses three or four times. What is their message? Consider committing these verses to memory over the next week.

RESPOND

When you think of all you have learned about consistent community in this session, what is one big lesson that has locked into your heart or one specific action that will impact your life?

PRAY

Close your group time by praying in any of the following directions:

- Thank God for the people in your life who have lived as an example of loving Christian community.
- Praise our trinitarian God for his eternal community within the Godhead and for his example of perfect community.

- Thank Jesus for his example of seeking community with the outcast and abandoned of his day, and pray for the courage to do the same in the community where you live.
- Pray that you will be an active and unifying presence in the church you call home.
- Ask Jesus to help you notice nonbelievers who are longing for community, and ask the Holy Spirit to guide you to invite them into your heart, home, church, social life, or some other aspect of the community you experience.
- Commit to God that you will seek to make your church a place of welcome and community for anyone who comes to visit.

Adventures in Organic Discipleship

Go deeper into the material you have covered in this session by engaging in the following between-session learning experiences. Each week, you will find four practical and life-impacting experiences you can engage in to go deeper as a disciple.

— Learn More (Growing your mind as a disciple) —

LIFE TOGETHER

Life Together, a classic book by Dietrich Bonhoeffer, is a small but powerful collection of reflections exploring Christian community. If you want to dig deeper into this topic, consider reading this book.

> God does not exist in isolation. God exists as three eternal persons, Father, Son, and Holy Spirit. One in being, existing in perfect unity as three persons—God is perfect community.

—— Live More (Developing spiritual disciplines) ——

A RHYTHM OF COMMUNITY

In a busy and fragmented world, establishing a rhythm of community is essential. Being part of a small group is a great way to do this. Attending worship services is also a great blessing. List five or six ways you can develop a weekly, monthly, or quarterly rhythm of gathering with Christian friends and cotravelers.

Ideas for regular community with believers:

Choose one of these to add to the rhythm of your spiritual life, and invite some others to join in. You'll be glad you did, and so will they.

—— Lead More (Investing in the next generation) ——

A CUP OF COFFEE

During one of our sons' adolescent years, as we were discipling and influencing him to take steps forward in faith, I (Sherry) would occasionally take him out for coffee. I was not a coffee drinker, but he liked it. He was into different coffee beverages, so I would treat, he would join me, and we forged conversation, connection, and community.

As you think about some of the people God has called you to influence, disciple, or mentor, plan to have a cup of coffee, share a meal, or have dessert with that person. There is something powerful about table fellowship. Use this time to share what God is teaching you, pray together, ask about their spiritual journey, and cheer them on in their growth as a Jesus follower.

> In a busy and hectic world, Christians need to rediscover the power of lingering over a meal with brothers and sisters in faith. Share life by praying for each other, telling stories, and laughing and crying together.

— Love More (Sharing Jesus' love, grace, and truth) —

PLAN A MEAL

Plan a barbecue or a meal of some kind that your whole group could put on and host. Have each member or couple in your group invite a person or a couple they care about who are not yet followers of Jesus. Now, here's the key. Don't get weird. Don't make it super religious. Don't stand around in a circle and ask everyone to lift up a thank-you prayer. Just share a meal, enjoy each other, make some introductions, laugh, meet some new folks, and see what Jesus does! If someone asks how you all know each other, tell them you are in a study group together. If they ask what you are studying, share it. But let God guide the conversation.

Organic Outreach

Love as I Have Loved You

God is always the first to reach out. He so loved the world that he gave his only Son. When Jesus walked this earth, he extended grace to every person he met. We who follow Jesus are to love people as he does. As his disciples, we carry the best news in human history. Our calling is to share the love and gospel of Jesus freely, in the power of the Spirit. As we partner with the Savior, he draws people to himself, and he alone receives the glory.

— Welcome —

It seems like every business, company, or organization these days has a simple statement of why they exist. They want to crystalize their mission so that everyone understands why they do what they do. Often, these brief and poignant declarations can keep an organization focused.

Lots of churches create mission statements, and they can be valuable as they clarify God's plan for their ministry. Here are three examples of mission statements:

1. Inspiring people to follow Jesus and fearlessly change the world
2. Loving God and loving people
3. To help as many people as possible become totally committed to Jesus Christ

You get the idea. Mission statements are a way to declare in one phrase or brief sentence who we are and what we do.

This concept is nothing new. More than two thousand years ago, Jesus did the same thing. Listen closely to Jesus' single-sentence summary of why he came into the world: "For the Son of Man came to seek and to save the lost" (Luke 19:10).

Short, sweet, and powerful! Jesus was saying, "Here is why I came to this world: I am all about seeking and saving the lost."

As his followers, we should find out what Jesus focused on and make it our passion. Jesus loves lost sheep. His heart breaks for them. He came not just to offer a vague idea of salvation. He left glory to look for us. To find us. To save lost people and bring them home to his love and grace.

> **Jesus came with the singular purpose of seeking and saving lost people—at the cost of his own life.**

— Share —

Tell about how you came to understand the story of Jesus' life, death, and resurrection. Describe how you placed your faith in Jesus and began following him.

— Watch —

Play the video for session 8 of the *Organic Disciples* small group experience. (These are free at www.OrganicDisciples.org/SmallGroupResources.) As you watch, use the following outline to record any thoughts, questions, or key points that stand out to you.

The evangelist of all evangelists

- Jesus' heart

- Jesus' mission

> The resurrection is the divine exclamation point after the crucifixion. All that Jesus promised was authenticated when he stood up and walked out of the grave.

Overcoming our fears

- Why is sharing our faith so nerve-wracking and challenging?

- How our identity gives us boldness for the mission

- God's part and our part

- Facing our fears

- Knowing our theology

- Counting the cost

Learning to do the thing we most want to do

- When our hearts and our actions don't line up

- Take it personally.

- Your story

- His story

> When Christians know who Jesus is at the core of his being, we gain clarity on how to serve and follow him. His names reveal his character and mission.

— Discuss —

With your group, discuss what you have just watched and explore these concepts in Scripture. Use the following questions to guide your discussion.

1. Talk about how one of the following names for Jesus gives you a window into his character and his mission to save lost people.
   > Messiah (John 4:25–26)

> Bread of Heaven (John 6:48–58)

> Living Water (John 7:37–38)

> The Light of the World (John 1:9–13)

> The Lamb of God (John 1:29)

> The Good Shepherd (John 10:11)

> The Gate (John 10:7–10)

> The Resurrection and the Life (John 11:25)

Read: John 11:25–26, 38–44. Jesus is the resurrection and the life! Why is Jesus' resurrection central to our faith? Why is confidence in his power to raise us from the dead also essential to the Christian message?

2. **Read:** 1 Corinthians 15:50–57. What did Jesus accomplish through his life, death, and resurrection? Since this is true, what message do we have for a world that is broken, fearful, anxious, and conflicted?

> Jesus emptied himself and came as one of us. He did it for sinful and broken people. For his beloved. For you.

3. Think about a person you love who has not yet embraced the message and grace of Jesus. How do you think this person's life could change if they opened their eyes, saw Jesus in his glory, received his grace, and followed him as the leader of their whole life?

4. **Read:** Matthew 28:19–20 and Acts 1:8. Jesus called his followers to tell lost people about his love, grace, and truth. Why do so many Christians struggle to fulfill this clear call of their Savior? Dig deep here: What gets in the way of our sharing our faith with joyful frequency?

5. In the same way that knowing Jesus' identity deepens our understanding of his mission, knowing who we are in Christ does the same for us. When you look at the way Jesus described his followers, what do you learn about your calling and mission?

   > You are a fisher of people (Mark 1:16–20).

   > You are a bearer of living water (John 4:13–14).

   > You are the light of the world (Matt. 5:14–16).

   > You are the salt of the earth (Matt. 5:13).

Which of these do you need to embrace and believe? How can your group pray for you to live into this identity?

> # Every day becomes an opportunity to shine the light of Jesus and share his gospel.

6. What is one fear you face as you think about sharing or seek to share the message and love of Jesus with others? What has helped you overcome some of your fears about or resistance to evangelism?

7. Amazing power is unleashed when a Christian tells the story of how they became a follower of Jesus. Within our stories is always the story of Jesus. Share your story with your group. How did you learn about each of these:
   > God's love for you

> Your need for forgiveness

> God's solution to your sin problem

> Your need to receive the amazing grace of Jesus

Our stories are different and amazing. As you share your story with your group, be sure to talk about how Jesus has transformed your life in wonderful ways.

READ AND REFLECT

Each session, you will be given a key verse to learn from one of the passages covered in the video teaching. This week, your suggested verse is Luke 19:10:

> For the Son of Man came to seek and to save the lost.
>
> **—LUKE 19:10**

Silently or as a group, read this verse three or four times. What is its message? Consider committing this verse to memory over the next week.

RESPOND

When you think of all you have learned about organic outreach in this session, what is one big lesson that has locked into your heart or one specific action that will impact your life?

PRAY

Close your group time by praying in any of the following directions:

- Thank God for reaching out to you and drawing you to his heart by the leading of the Holy Spirit.
- Praise God for the gift of grace revealed in Jesus and for the people who shared the life-changing story of Jesus with you.
- Ask God to make Jesus' mission the consuming passion of your life.
- Pray that you will learn to see lost and wandering people just like Jesus does: as sheep without a shepherd.
- Invite the Holy Spirit to show you where you have let fear enter your heart and keep you from reaching out to people with the grace and message of Jesus.
- Commit to learn one new way to share the story of Jesus, and ask God to give you opportunities to share the Good News.

Adventures in Organic Discipleship

Go deeper into the material you have covered in this session by engaging in the following after-session learning experiences to help you go deeper as a disciple.

—— Learn More (Growing your mind as a disciple) ——

ORGANIC OUTREACH

If you want to dig into what it looks like to shine Jesus' light in natural ways in the everyday flow of your life, consider reading the book *Organic Outreach for Ordinary People: Sharing Good News Naturally*. We wrote it for the 97 percent of Christians who are not gifted as evangelists but want to shine Jesus' light in the flow of their lives.

—— Live More (Developing spiritual disciplines) ——

REGULAR AND PASSIONATE PRAYERS

List all the people you love who are still far from God. Keep this list in a journal or a private note in your phone. After the list of names, write down these prayer ideas:

1. God of love, soften their hearts to your grace and care.
2. Lord of power, silence the enemy and remove his influence in their lives.
3. Spirit of God, tenderly draw them to yourself.
4. Heavenly Father, bring your children home to your arms and heart.
5. Lord Jesus, give me courage to join you on your mission of seeking and saving each of these people.
6. Lord of the harvest, send more and more workers into your harvest fields, starting with me.

> In God's heart, there are only two kinds of people: those whom God loves and delights in because they have come to him through faith in Jesus, and those whom God loves who have not yet come home to him. That's it!

— Lead More (Investing in the next generation) —

PRACTICE TOGETHER

When you are with a Christian you are helping to grow deeper in faith, practice telling each other your stories of how you became followers of Jesus. As you do, be sure to tell Jesus' story and include these four elements:

1. God's love for you
2. Your need for forgiveness of sin
3. God's solution to your sin problem
4. Your need to receive the amazing grace of Jesus

You can let each other know what parts of your stories really made sense and connected, and what parts could use more detail or clarity. It is amazing how practicing sharing our stories with other Christians prepares us to share naturally with those who are not yet following Jesus. As you share, always include a few thoughts about how Jesus has transformed your life in wonderful ways as you continue to follow him every day of your life.

—— Love More (Sharing Jesus' love, grace, and truth) ——

GROWING FEARLESS

One of the best ways to defeat fear is to face it, to know your enemy. Take time to thoughtfully and prayerfully reflect on what you are afraid of when it comes to sharing your faith with others. Use the following space to take notes that will help guide you to a process of prayer about these things.

When you think about sharing with others that you are a Christian and that you really do love Jesus, what are you afraid of? What do you think could happen?

When you think about telling the story of Jesus' life, death, resurrection, love, and offer of forgiveness (sharing the gospel), what are you afraid of? What do you think could happen?

Bring each of these fears to God and ask him to remove the lies, reduce your anxiety, and give you clear thinking and a bold heart to grow in your organic outreach.

Closing Thoughts

Nothing is more meaningful and joyful than drawing close to the God who made us and loves us. When the fruit of the Spirit is growing in us and forming our character, we become more like Jesus. As we join in the great procession of Christians throughout history and lock hands with people in front of us and behind us, we become true disciples. We learn from those who are more mature. We take consistent steps of growth. We help others go deeper in faith. And we teach them to take the hand of the next generation and do the same. This is the pathway of organic disciples.

Each day, our journey is upward to God as worshipers, inward toward his family in community, and outward to the world with the gospel. Every one of the markers of spiritual maturity connects us to God, makes us more like Jesus, and propels us out to love the lost sheep that Jesus came to save.

Follow Jesus.

Enjoy the climb.

Never travel alone.

Lock hands and press on for the glory of God!

—In the joy of Jesus,
Kevin and Sherry Harney

Leading This Group

GROUP SIZE

The Organic Disciples Study Guide is designed to be experienced in a group setting such as a Bible study, Sunday school class, or any small group gathering. To ensure everyone has enough time to participate in discussions, it is recommended that large groups break up into smaller groups of four to six people each.

MATERIALS NEEDED

Each participant should have his or her own study guide, which includes notes for video segments, directions for activities, and discussion questions, as well as personal studies to deepen learning between sessions.

TIMING

Each session will take between ninety minutes and two hours. For those who have less time available to meet, you can use fewer questions for discussion.

FACILITATION

Each group should appoint a facilitator who is responsible for starting the video and keeping track of time during discussions and activities. Facilitators may also read questions aloud and monitor discussions, prompting participants to respond and assuring that everyone has the opportunity to participate. The facilitator should also guide the group members through the prayer prompts and encourage them to dig into the four activities provided at the end of each session.

PERSONAL STUDIES

Maximize the impact of the curriculum with additional study between group sessions. There are four practical experiences provided following each session. Feel free to engage with these optional study materials as much or as little as you need.

Recommended Resources

— Books and Video Studies —

- *Organic Disciples* (Kevin G. Harney and Sherry Harney)
- The Organic Outreach trilogy:
  - *Organic Outreach for Ordinary People* (Kevin G. Harney)
  - *Organic Outreach for Churches* (Kevin G. Harney)
  - *Organic Outreach for Families* (Kevin G. Harney and Sherry Harney)
- *Organic Outreach for Ordinary People Video Study*
- *Organic Outreach for Churches Video Study*

— Online Resources for Evangelism and Discipleship —

The following are available at www.OrganicOutreach.org:

- Church Outreach Culture Assessment
- Seven Markers of Spiritual Growth Assessment
- Outreach Infusion Curriculum (free in English and Spanish): go to Resources / Outreach Influence Team Resources / Outreach Influence Infusions.
- Organic Outreach Podcasts: go to Resources / Organic Outreach Podcast.
- Organic Outreach Newsletter

For great resources to go deeper into organic disciples and outreach, go to the Organic Outreach website: https://www.OrganicOutreach.org/.
If you have questions, please contact the Organic Outreach offices: 831-655-1329.